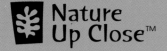

Spiders Up Close

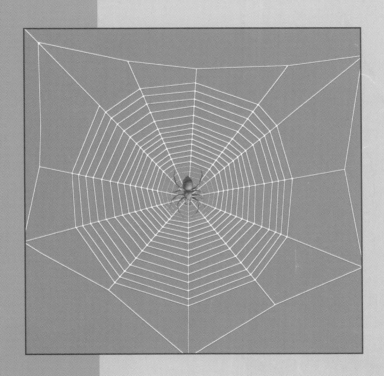

PowerKiDS press
New York

Katie Franks

Published in 2008 by The Rosen Publishing Group, Inc.
29 East 21st Street, New York, NY 10010

First Edition

Editor: Jennifer Way
Book Design: Kate Laczynski
Photo Researcher: Nicole Pristash

Photo Credits: Cover, pp. 1, 5, 7, 9, 11, 13, 15, 19, 21, 23, 24 © Studio Stalio; pp. 13, 23 Shutterstock.com; p. 17 © www.istockphoto.com/Alexander V. Chelmodeev.

Library of Congress Cataloging-in-Publication Data

Franks, Katie.
  Spiders up close / Katie Franks. — 1st ed.
      p. cm. — (Nature up close)
  Includes index.
  ISBN 978-1-4042-4138-1 (library binding)
  1. Spiders—Juvenile literature. I. Title.
  QL458.4.F73 2008
  595.4'4—dc22
                                          2007019152

Manufactured in the United States of America

Contents

Spiders are small animals that have eight legs. Spiders are known for spinning sticky webs.

Spiders have many body parts. A few of these parts are the mouth, eyes, legs, **stomach**, heart, and **spinnerets**.

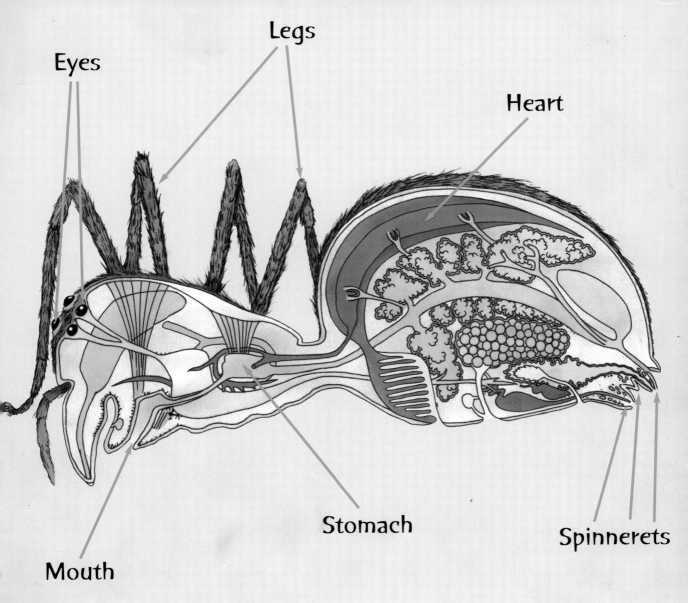

Eyes

Legs

Heart

Mouth

Stomach

Spinnerets

7

The spinnerets are special body parts on the underside of a spider. Spiders use their spinnerets to build webs.

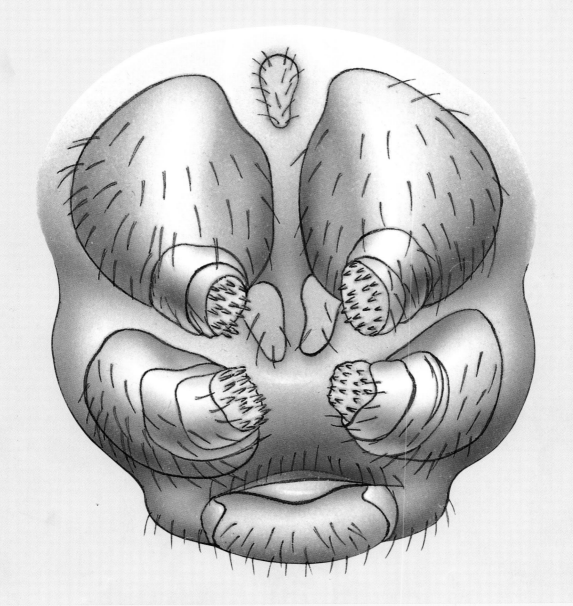

9

There are many steps to building a web. All webs start with just one **thread**!

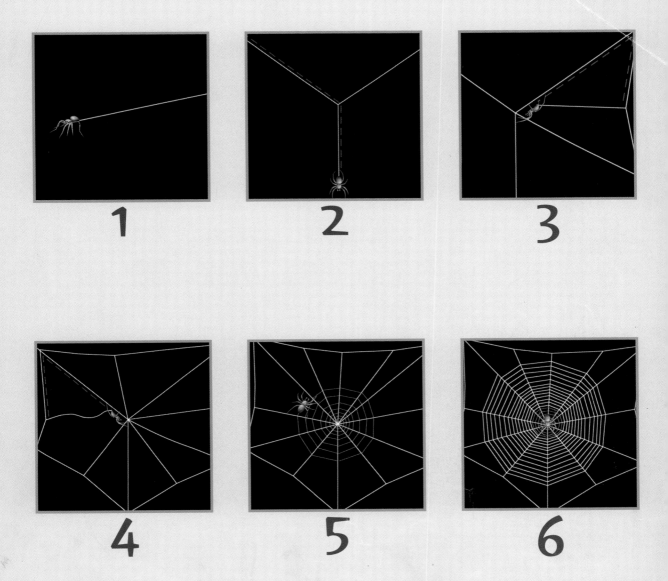

There are many different kinds of webs. This is an orb web. Each type of spider spins its own kind of web.

Spiders use their webs to trap their food. Spiders eat bugs and small animals.

15

Spiders are eaten by some kinds of bugs and small animals. This spider is being eaten by a praying mantis.

Female, or girl, spiders lay eggs. The eggs are kept together in an egg sac.

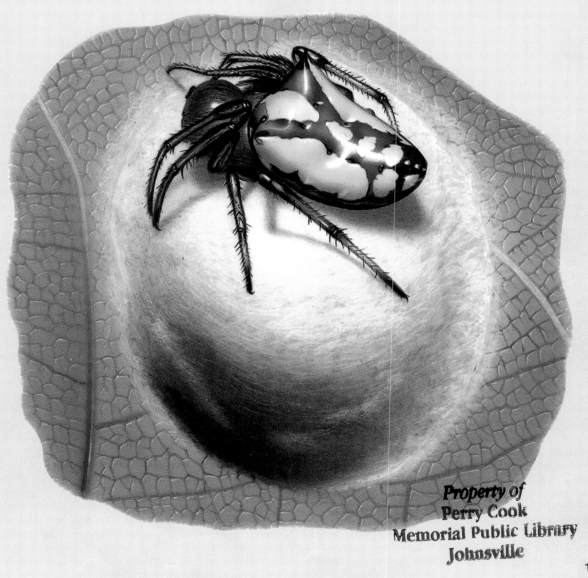

19

Baby spiders grow by **molting**. When it molts, the spider's old skin comes off and a new, larger skin takes its place.

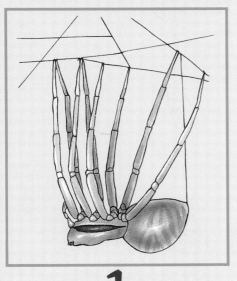

1

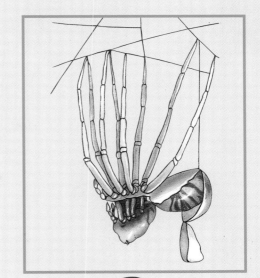

2

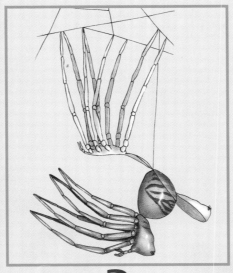

3

This is a huntsman spider.
It lives in Australia. Spiders live
in just about every country in
the world!

Words to Know

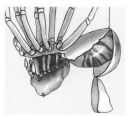
molting

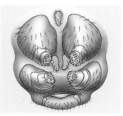
spinnerets

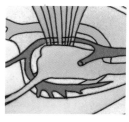
stomach

thread

Index

Web Sites

Due to the changing nature of Internet links, PowerKids Press has developed an online list of Web sites related to the subject of this book. This site is updated regularly. Please use this link to access the list: www.powerkidslinks.com/nuc/spider/